DATE DUE

Materials, Materials, Materials

Glass

Chris Oxlade

Heinemann Library
Chicago, Illinois

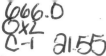
© 2001 Reed Educational & Professional Publishing
Published by Heinemann Library,
an imprint of Reed Educational & Professional Publishing,
Chicago, Illinois

Customer Service 888-454-2279

Visit our website at www.heinemannlibrary.com

Designed by Storeybooks
Originated by Ambassador Litho Ltd.
Printed in Hong Kong / China

05 04 03 02 01
10 9 8 7 6 5 4 3 2 1

Library of Congress Cataloging-in-Publication Data

Oxlade, Chris.
   Glass / by Chris Oxlade.
      p. cm. -- (Materials, materials, materials)
Includes bibliographical references and index.
   ISBN 1-58810-154-1
   1. Glass--Juvenile literature. [1. Glass.] I. Title. II. Series.
   TP857.3 .O8 2001
   666.1--dc21

                              00-012890

Acknowledgments
The author and publishers are grateful to the following for permission to reproduce copyright material:
Corbis/James L. Amos, p. 4; Tudor Photography, pp. 5, 22; Powerstock Zefa, pp. 6, 11; Corbis/William J. Warren, p. 7; Corbis/Nik Wheeler, p. 8; Abode, p. 9; Corbis/Vince Streano, p. 10; Corbis/H. David Seawell, p. 12; Pilkington, p. 13; Science Photo Library/Victor de Schwanberg, p. 14; Corbis/Phil Schermeister, p. 15; Barnaby's Picture Library, p. 16; Crafts Council/Jane McDonald, p. 17; Trip/S. Grant, p. 18; Science Photo Library/Pascal Goetgheluck, p. 19; View/Dennis Gilbert, p. 20; View/Philip Bier, p. 23; Corbis/Lawrence Manning, p. 24; PPL Library, p. 25; Bruce Coleman Collection/Pacific Stock, p. 26; Oxford Scientific Films/Colin Monteath, p. 27; Corbis p. 29.

Cover photograph reproduced with permission of Tudor Photography.

Every effort has been made to contact copyright holders of any material reproduced in this book. Any omissions will be rectified in subsequent printings if notice is given to the publisher.

Note to the Reader
Some words are shown in bold, **like this.**
You can find out what they mean by looking in the glossary.

Contents

What Is Glass?

Glass is a material that people make in **factories.** It is not a **natural** material. These thin sheets of glass have just been made. They will be used as windows.

Glass is an important material. It is waterproof and see-through. We make many things from glass. All the things in this picture are made of glass.

Breaking Glass

Glass breaks easily if it is dropped or hit by something. It often breaks into big, sharp pieces. People can get hurt by broken glass.

Glass for windows is made to be stronger. If it breaks, the pieces will be tiny and round. Or it may crack and not break. This type of glass is called safety glass.

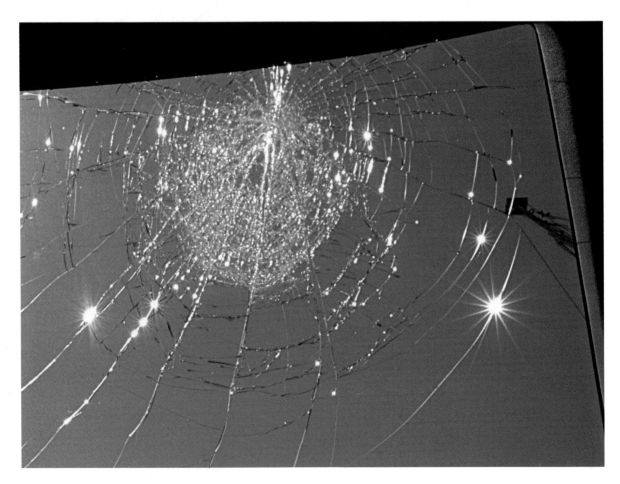

See-Through Glass

All glass lets light through it. Some glass is see-through. It is easy for you to look through it. See-through glass may be clear or colored.

Some glass is **opaque.** It lets light in, but you cannot see through it. Bathroom windows are often opaque so that no one can see inside.

Heat and Chemicals

Glass does not catch on fire when it is heated. Firefighters wear clothes made with thin **fibers** of glass to protect them from flames.

Strong **chemicals** will damage metal or plastic. But glass is not affected by most chemicals. So, scientists store most chemicals in glass bottles and tubes.

Making Glass

Glass is made from sand like you would see on a beach. The sand is mixed with other **chemicals.** Then it is heated. When it gets very, very, hot, it **melts** into a thick liquid.

When the hot liquid cools, it hardens as glass. To make thin sheets of glass, the liquid is spread over hot, liquid metal in a special machine.

Shaping Glass

Some glass objects are made in **molds.**
Hot, liquid glass is poured into a mold.
When the glass has cooled, the new
object can be taken out of the mold.

Some glass objects are blown into shape.
A glass blower puts hot, liquid glass on
the end of a tube. He blows into the
tube. The glass blows up like a balloon.
When it cools, it keeps its new shape.

Making Patterns

You can decorate glass by making
patterns on its surface. This artist is
using a cutting tool to make patterns
on a glass bottle.

You also can make patterns by **etching.** Patterns are painted onto the glass with **chemicals.** They eat away at the surface of the glass. A pattern is left when the chemicals are wiped off.

Mirrors and Lenses

A mirror is made from a sheet of glass. The back of the glass is covered with silver paint. Light goes into the glass and bounces off the paint. Then it goes back out again.

A magnifying glass is made from a piece of glass called a lens. The lens is thicker in the middle than at the edges. This bends light and makes things look bigger than they really are.

Glass in Buildings

Glass windows let sunlight into buildings.
They keep heat inside buildings during
the winter. They also help keep cool air
inside buildings during the summer.

In places with cold winters, many buildings have a special kind of windows. Each window has two sheets of glass with a small gap between them. This helps keep wind, rain, and cold air outside.

Looking Good

Glass can look very pretty when light bounces off of it. People sometimes cut glass into small shapes to make jewelry.

Small pieces of stained, or colored, glass are used to make patterns. **Stained glass** windows look beautiful when sunlight shines through them.

High-Tech Glass

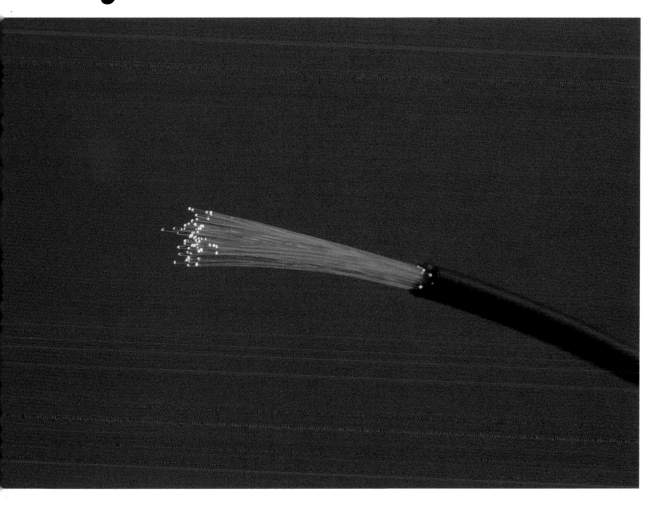

This cable has long, thin glass **fibers** inside. Flashes of light travel along them carrying telephone calls. They are called **optical fibers.**

This boat is being made from **fiberglass.** Fiberglass is made by mixing fibers of glass and plastic. It is stronger than either glass or plastic would be alone.

Recycling Glass

Bottles, jars, and other glass things can be **recycled.** Most recycling centers have bins where you can drop off glass.

The glass things are taken to a **factory.**
There the glass is cleaned, sorted by
color, and broken into pieces. Then it
is **melted** and made into new things.

Fact File

- Glass has to be made. It is not a **natural** material.

- Regular glass breaks into pieces easily. Safety glass is stronger than regular glass.

- Glass lets light through. It can be clear or colored.

- Glass does not burn. It becomes a liquid only when it gets very, very hot.

- Glass is waterproof. It does not **rot.**

- **Electricity** does not flow through glass.

- Heat flows through glass, but not very well. A layer of **fiberglass** is often used to keep heat inside buildings.

- Glass is not attracted by **magnets.**

Can You Believe It?

Some of the biggest glass things in the world are the mirrors in **telescopes.** The biggest mirror is six and a half yards (six meters) across. That is as wide as three adults lying down in a row!

Glossary

chemical material used to clean or protect something

electricity form of power that can light lamps, heat houses, and make things work

etching making a pattern on a surface by letting chemicals eat away at it

factory place where things are made using machines

fiber very thin thread or small piece of material as thin as one of your hairs

fiberglass glass threads that can be mixed with plastic to make a strong material or can be used to make a material that keeps houses warm

magnet piece of iron or steel that pulls iron and steel things toward it

melt turn from solid to liquid

mold shape into which liquid material is poured in order to form it

natural comes from plants, animals, or rocks in the earth

opaque not see-through, looks frosty or foggy

optical fiber strand of glass that carries telephone calls, fax messages, and e-mail

recycle to use a material again, often to make new things

rot to fall apart because of dampness

stained glass glass that has been colored by melting it and mixing it with colored dye

telescope machine with a special lens that allows scientists to look into space

More Books to Read

Gibbons, Gail. *Recycle!: A Handbook for Kids*. New York: Little, Brown & Co., 1996.

Madgwick, Wendy. *Super Materials*. Austin, Tex.: Raintree Steck-Vaughn, 1999.

Purcell, Cindy. *From Glass to Boat*. Danbury, Conn.: Children's Press, 1998.

Warbrick, Sarah. *What Is See-Through?* Chicago: Heinemann Library, 1998.

Index